FRAM
To the Ends of the Earth

Christopher Routledge

Long Lane Press

First Published 2011
Long Lane Press
31, Long Lane
Ormskirk, L39 5AS

longlanepress.co.uk

Copyright © 2011 Christopher Routledge

The right of Christopher Routledge to be identified as the author of this work has been asserted by him in accordance with the Copyright, Designs and Patents Act, 1988.

Some rights reserved. This book is licensed under a **Creative Commons Attribution-NonCommercial-ShareAlike 3.0 Unported License.** http://creativecommons.org/licenses/by-nc-sa/3.0/

British Library Cataloguing-in-Publication Data
A British Library CIP Record is available.

ISBN: 978-0-9568878-0-1

Contents

Introduction	1
FRAM: Forward	3
The South Pole	15
The Voyage of the *Fram*	23
Fram Timeline	33
Technical Data	37
Bibliography	39

Illustrations

P. 1. *Fram* leaving Bergen, by Fridtjof Nansen. From Nansen's book *Farthest North*, 1897.

P. 8. The saloon of the *Fram*, by Fridtjof Nansen. From Nansen's book *Farthest North*, 1897.

P. 23, P. 30. Images of *Fram* in the ice in Antarctica, by Roald Amundsen. From Amundsen's *The South Pole*, 1912.

P. 37. Designs for Nansen's Arctic exploration vessel *Fram*. From Fridtjof Nansen's book, *Farthest North*, 1897.

All other images © Christopher Routledge.

Introduction

In the years before World War I, the Norwegian polar expeditionary ship *Fram*, held the record for the farthest north and farthest south achieved by any vessel, and still holds the record for a wooden ship.

Built for five-year long voyages, and for overwintering in the harshest Arctic weather, *Fram*, meaning 'Forward,' was involved in three of the most dramatic of all polar adventures: first an attempt on the North Pole, under the command of Fridtjof Nansen, then Otto Sverdrup's stay at Ellesmere Island, and finally, Roald Amundsen's 'race' to the South Pole in 1910-1912. Norway celebrates its explorers, but their monuments are their ships: Viking longships, the *Kon-Tiki*, and the *Fram*, beset for the last time, in concrete, on the peninsula of Bygdøy, in Oslo Fjord.

After Nansen's return alive from the Arctic in 1896, the *Fram* was a famous ship in Norway. But when Amundsen's success at reaching the South Pole became known, in March 1912, the name '*Fram*' became familiar around the world. Only the sinking of the *Titanic* the following month made another 'indestructible' ship more famous. Wherever the expedition put in on its way home, from Hobart to Buenos Aires, the quaysides were full of sightseers, tourists, and journalists. The story of Amundsen's race for the Pole is well known; less often told is the story of the *Fram*, 'Norway's own ship'.

FRAM: Forward

On 14 December, 1911, after a two month trek from the Eastern Ross Ice Barrier (now known as the Ross Ice Shelf), Roald Amundsen reached the South Pole with his Norwegian team of four, beating the British expedition, led by Captain Robert Scott, which arrived at the Pole on 17 January. Scott, of course, did not survive the homeward journey. He and his men perished on the ice, leaving behind the sad detritus of a mission that was disadvantaged from the start by inadequate equipment, ineffective planning, and the mistake of choosing ponies rather than dogs for pulling sledges. Delays on the way to the Barrier meant that after reaching the Pole, Scott, and his four companions were overtaken by bad weather, and ran out of supplies.

The obsessive thoroughness of Amundsen has become part of the mythology of polar exploration, a mythology Amundsen himself was keen to exploit. He was undoubtedly lucky with the weather, but he wrote in *The South Pole* (1912), his book about the expedition, that the greatest factor in the success of any mission was "the way in which the expedition is equipped—the way in which every difficulty is foreseen, and precautions taken for meeting, or avoiding it. Victory awaits him who has everything in order" (*The South Pole*, 212). Amundsen was not the first Norwegian explorer to have an obsession with detail and planning; nor did he work in isolation. Amundsen's Antarctic expedition was indebted to the work of Fridtjof Nansen, 20 years earlier. In particular, Amundsen had Nansen to thank for the design of his ship.

Before the *Fram*, few expeditionary ships were purpose built. Most were converted whalers, or naval vessels. But when Nansen began planning his attempt to reach the North Pole, in the 1880s, he realised he would need a different kind of ship; a ship of unprecedented strength and resilience. Nansen intended to use the east-west drift of the polar ice sheet, theorised by the meteorologist Henrik Mohn, to carry *Fram* and her crew from Siberia, across the North Pole, to Greenland. It was an audacious idea, which challenged orthodox thinking about Arctic exploration, and ship design. After he announced his intention, in 1890, many people thought such a mission would end in disaster.

An east-west current across the Arctic region had long been suspected, though it remained unconfirmed. As far back as 1822, the British whaler William Scoresby Jr. had observed tree trunks in the Greenland Sea, and concluded, with good reason, that they must have come from Siberia:

"A great quantity of drift-wood was passed during the day. Sometimes two or three pieces were seen at once. We picked up two trees, one of which was above thirty feet in length, perfectly straight, and well adapted for a jib-boom. This great supply of drift-wood is probably derived from some of the extensive rivers in Siberia, which empty themselves into the Frozen

Ocean; and being carried by the westerly current, prevailing on this coast, is dispersed throughout the Greenland Sea." (Scoresby, 1823: 19)

Scoresby backed up his theory that the driftwood came from Siberia by examining the age of the trees, their slow growth indicating that they came from high latitudes. Further, and more recent, evidence that this might be possible came primarily from the remains of the American expeditionary ship the *Jeanette*, which was lost in the summer of 1881, off Siberia. Identifiable items from the wreck of the *Jeanette* were found, some years later, on the coast of Greenland.

Nansen was convinced that the ice would carry his ship, just as it had carried the remains of the *Jeanette*, across the top of the world. His plan required a small, lightweight vessel that would be home to 12 men for up to five years. The ship would also have to be extremely strong. With funding from the Norwegian government, and private sponsors, Nansen commissioned the *Fram* from Norwegian shipbuilder Colin Archer. Between them they developed specifications that would enable the ship to withstand long periods beset, or trapped by ice, and to support its crew during that time.

The inspiration for the design came from the small boats used by fishermen in the north of Norway, boats with curved hulls designed not to resist the ice, but rise up out of it as it pressed against them. *Fram*, of course, was a much larger vessel, and would have to be built light as well as strong. Nansen wrote: "The sides must

slope sufficiently to prevent the ice, when it presses together, from getting a firm hold on the hull, as was the case with the *Jeanette*, and other vessels. Instead of nipping the ship, the ice must raise it out of the water" (*Farthest North*, 22). Despite criticism from other shipbuilders, and a widespread view that Nansen's planned expedition was suicidal, Nansen and Archer went ahead with the design. Nansen was confident they could build the ship: "No very new departure in construction is likely to be needed, for the *Jeanette*, notwithstanding her preposterous build, was able to hold out against the ice pressure for about two years" (*Farthest North*, 22). *Fram* was launched at Archer's shipyard at Larvik, on October 6, 1892.

Scepticism about the *Fram*'s design centred on its deviation from a shipbuilding consensus going back back a century or more. In the nineteenth century, Britain dominated Arctic exploration, and the search for the Northwest Passage, notably through the expeditions of John Ross, William Parry, and John Franklin. Arctic exploration had been undertaken mostly by expeditions commissioned and funded by the Admiralty, using adapted naval supply vessels, or ships designed along similar lines. While some important discoveries were made by Arctic whalers, in particular by William Scoresby Jr., even the promise of large bounties had not persuaded whalers to undertake sustained exploration. Meanwhile, the over-supply of ships and naval personnel, in the years following the Napoleonic Wars, meant that the British navy had the resources for exploration, as well as an incentive to widen British influence and control. In this conservative atmosphere, in which ships

and manpower were plentiful, purpose-built expeditionary ships were rare.

By the 1880s, as whale stocks dwindled, there were plenty of redundant or retired whale ships available, and they were much cheaper to fit out for expeditions than vessels built from scratch. Whale ships had many attributes required for research and exploration. They were capable cargo vessels, good sailors in open water, and nimble amongst the ice, even when heavily loaded. But while they were undoubtedly strong, standard whale ships were vulnerable to being crushed, and had to be modified for expeditionary work. Arctic whalers did not overwinter if they could help it, and tried to avoid being beset.

With the addition of steam power, and harpoon guns, whalers in the 1880s were considerably larger than they had been 60 years earlier. *Terra Nova*, Scott's ship in 1910-1912, was originally built in Dundee in 1884, as a whaler. With reinforcements and modifications, *Terra Nova* grossed 764 tons, almost twice the weight of the *Fram*. Scott described the *Terra Nova* as "a fine ice ship," and this tribute to the ship's strength is borne out by the fact that it was not until 1943 that *Terra Nova* was lost, still in service, off the coast of Greenland.

Like *Terra Nova*, the *Fram* was also heavily reinforced, with a retractable rudder, and screw, but unlike a whaler, *Fram* was not

built as an all-rounder. In his contribution to Amundsen's book *The South Pole* (1912), Commodore Christian Blom, superintendent of the Horten dockyard, emphasises the lack of compromise in the ship's design:

"The problem which it was sought to solve in the construction of the *Fram* was that of providing a ship which could survive the crushing embrace of the Arctic drift-ice. To fit her for this was the object before which all considerations had to give way." (*The South Pole*, 404)

One of the consequences of this focus on a single aspect of the design is that *Fram* is a strange-looking, dumpy-shaped ship, a 'fore-and-aft' rigged schooner, just 39 metres (128 feet) long, and pointed at both ends, with upturned prow and stern. *Fram* is a small ship, built solid and strong, but also built, as Archer put it, to avoid impact rather than confront it. The design avoided flat plane surfaces, and gave the ship rounded sides, a curved bottom, and a keel almost invisible from the outside, so that horizontal pressure would push the ice under the hull, rather than against it.

Fram turned out to be much heavier than Nansen and Archer anticipated, but the ship's strength was exceptional. With a keel 35.5 centimetres (14 inches) square of American elm, and timbers arranged in two tiers, at 25.4 and 28 centimetres (10 and 11 inches) square, *Fram*'s framing is oversized. Iron armour covers the keel, the stern, and bow, while massive stays strengthen the ship's sides. An ice skin of greenheart oak covers the hull, which itself consists of a double layer of oak planking. Altogether, the thickness of the *Fram*'s sides is between 71 and 84 centimetres (28 and 33 inches), braced with iron. Smooth 'carvel' planking also resisted being torn away as it moved against the ice. The cabins were lined on the inside with cork insulation, reindeer fur, felt, and wood panelling, and to prevent the transmission of cold, and the development of condensation, no ironwork visible on the inside also protruded on the outside.

There were many predictions that that the *Fram* would be destroyed, and that no ship could ever escape, once gripped. In London, Admiral Sir Leopold Mclintock agreed with Nansen's theory about Arctic drift, but expressed the widely-held view that the *Fram* would never be seen again. Sir Joseph Hooker declared "I do not think that a ship, of whatever build, could long resist destruction if committed to the movements of the pack in the polar regions" (*Farthest North*, 32). Despite such eminent critics, Nansen remained convinced that a strong ship could ride the ice, possibly across the North Pole itself.

Unusually, for an Arctic expedition, Nansen set off in the autumn. *Fram* entered the ice off Siberia in September 1893, became trapped, according to the plan, and began to drift slowly north. Progress was very slow, but a year and a half later the expedition had reached 83° 47′ North, a new record. On March 14, 1895, Nansen, with Hjalmar Johansen, who later participated in Amundsen's South Pole expedition, set off with a dog team, aiming for the Pole. In the end they failed to reach the Pole, but set a new record of 86° 13′ North before turning back. Drifting slowly with the ice, *Fram* eventually reached 85° 55′ North before the ice began to move south again.

Speculation about the survival of the expedition continued. In March 1895, the *New York Times* reported the opinion of Lieutenant David L. Brainard, under the headline 'Will Nansen Come Back'. Brainard doubted that anyone would survive, arguing that the currents across the Pole were inconsistent, and that "When a ship once comes within the grip of ice of this kind, she never returns."

Nansen and Johansen struggled across the frozen sea, living off seals, and gulls, and feeding the dogs to each other to keep them going, and in the winter of 1895 they settled down in a rudimentary hut they built on Franz Josef Land. Meanwhile, the *Fram*, commanded by Otto Sverdrup, continued the slow drift westward. Nansen and Johansen somehow managed to survive the winter, and were rescued by Frederick Jackson, a British explorer. They joined his ship, the *Windward*, on August 7, 1896. The *Fram* was also on its way home, having survived the crushing force of the Arctic ice. Despite its weight, *Fram*'s ability to ride atop the ice had been demonstrated during three polar winters.

On August 21, after making landfall at Skjervøy the day before, *Fram* sailed into Tromsø, where Sverdrup and the crew were reunited with Nansen and Johansen. The expedition arrived back in Christiania (now Oslo) on September 9, where it was met by large crowds. The crew attended a reception with King Oscar, and Nansen stayed at the palace. However, Johansen received little recognition for his part in the expedition.

Although Nansen had failed to reach the

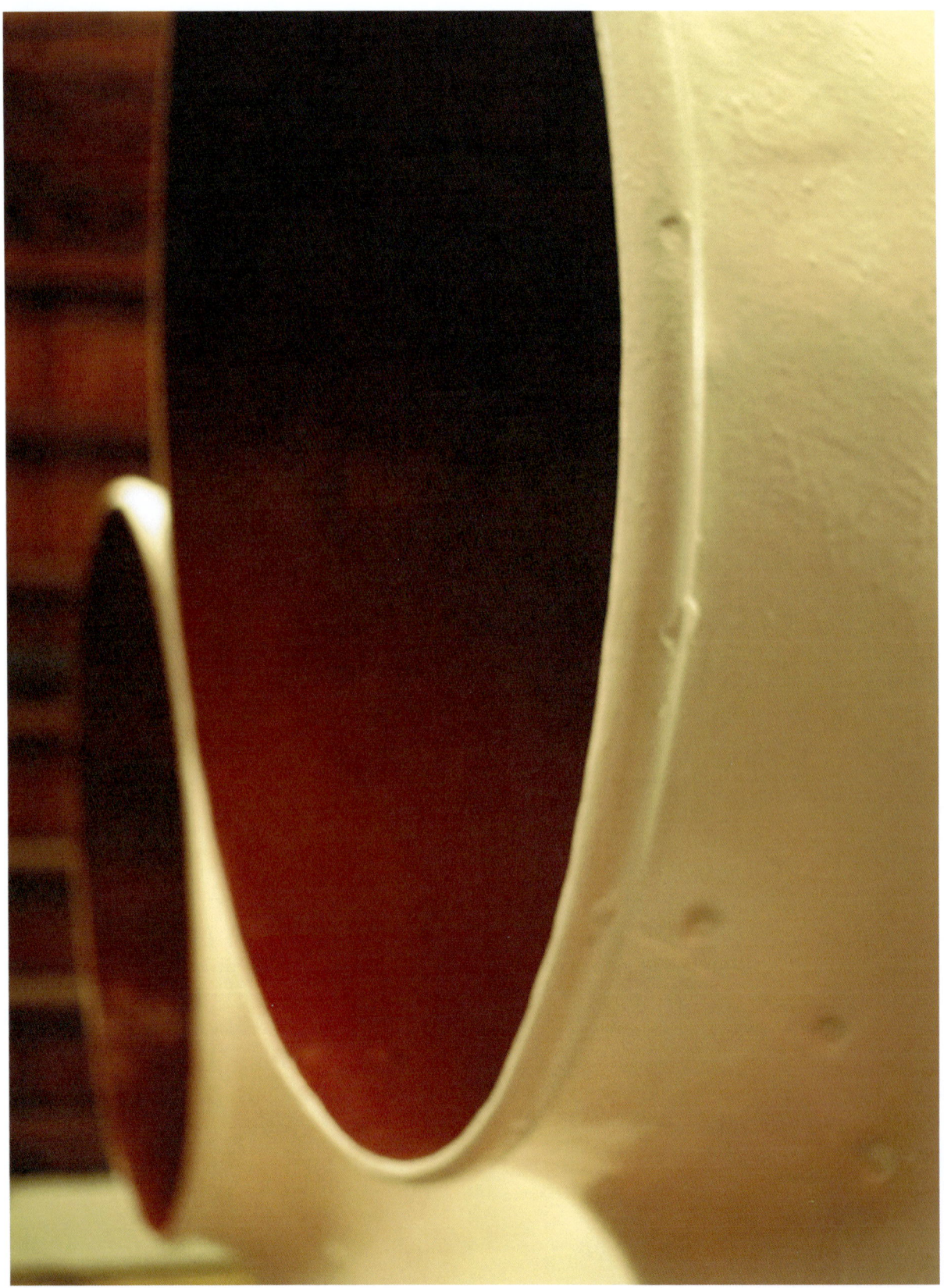

Pole, he had proved the theory of Arctic drift, and records kept on the *Fram* confirmed that the polar ice sheet floated on an ocean 2000 metres deep. Nansen's small scale approach to organising expeditions—it involved a crew of just 12 men—was later adopted by Amundsen in Antarctica, whose crew of 16 contrasted with the 65 who accompanied Scott.

The second voyage of the *Fram* was equally tough, supporting Sverdrup's own Arctic voyage in 1898. Sverdrup aimed to explore the Canadian Arctic islands, and hoped to find a route around Greenland. The expedition was detained by ice at Ellesmere Island, which lies at the head of Baffin Bay, to the west, and there Sverdrup and his crew overwintered, charting and naming several islands in the area. Although the expedition was supposed to last three years, in fact it lasted four. The *Fram* remained trapped in the ice until 1902.

This expedition yielded a great deal of information about the Arctic region, and thousands of plant, animal, and geological samples, including fossils. The expedition also surveyed 200,000 square kilometres of islands, claiming them for Norway. The whole area is now part of Canada.

After two ambitious expeditions, *Fram* might have become a footnote in Norway's tradition of polar exploration. On returning from Greenland, in 1902 the ship was laid up in the Horten Naval dockyard, and in 1905 became a floating magazine for the marine artillery. Blom describes how a fire in a storehouse on shore destroyed the rigging and sails. By then, *Fram* was in danger of becoming a hulk, useful only as a store until rot and decay took over. For a while there were plans to turn the ship into a floating museum, but they came to nothing.

The South Pole

In 1907 few would have predicted that the sorry-looking *Fram* would become part of one of the most famous of all polar expeditions, but in that year Amundsen was thinking about an attempt to reach the North Pole, and was looking for a ship. His plans changed when the Pole was claimed first by the discredited Frederick Cook in 1908, and then by Robert Peary, in 1909, but Amundsen kept his new goal, the South Pole, secret.

By 1907 it was widely assumed that *Fram* was beyond repair, but on inspection the ship was found to be in surprisingly good condition. Even so there was a great deal of superficial decay. Much of the reindeer hair and cork insulation had mouldered in the damp atmosphere, and some of the cabin ceilings were rotten. There was rot and fungus in parts of the deck timbers above, and parts of the masts had also succumbed.

Although some of the superstructure needed repair, *Fram*'s keel and stem had been sheathed in zinc in 1903, and the hull had been kept coated in tar, protecting it from the sea and the weather. *Fram* was stripped out, de-masted, and a thorough examination conducted. The whole of the rest of the ship was found to be strong and sound. Blom says:

"It is difficult to imagine any better proof of the excellence of the vessel's construction; after two protracted expeditions to the most northern regions to which any ship has ever penetrated, where the vessel was often exposed to the severest ice-pressure, and in spite of her being (in 1907) fifteen years old, the examination showed that her actual hull, the part of the ship that has to resist the heavy strain of water and ice, was in just as good condition as when she was new." (*The South Pole*, 409)

Amundsen's critics, most of whom had not inspected the *Fram*, insisted that the ship was leaky and rotten, but it was not the case. When Amundsen inspected *Fram*, on June 1st, 1908, he brought Colin Archer, the ship's creator, with him, and they concluded that the work required would not be prohibitive.

Fram was lent to the expedition by the Norwegian government, and KR75,000 (roughly £4,132) put forward for recommissioning. In March 1909 the dockyard agreed to make the necessary repairs, and design some modifications to the ship. Most significantly, they replaced the steam engine with a 180-horsepower diesel motor, and the necessary fuel tanks for 95 days' running. Combined with the sails, the engine allowed powered sailing over about 10,000 miles. But Although the diesel engine was an improvement on steam, it was not without its problems, and needed frequent attention to prevent the pistons coking up. The problem was eventually solved by changing the fuel from oil to paraffin.

Other changes were less obvious. The foremast was square rigged for easier

sailing over a long distance, though as Amundsen points out in his account of the voyage, lack of money meant that they had two sails on the foremast where there could have been four. Also upgraded were the insulation to the cabins, supports for the masts—the mizzen mast itself was replaced, but reused as a bowsprit—and a petroleum-fired heating system for the laboratory. The zinc sheathing which had helped protect the ship in harbour, was removed, for fear that it would prevent the ship slipping upwards through the ice, and a new, heavier anchor, weighing well over a ton, was added to the port side, for use around Cape Horn.

Blom concludes his account of the renovation with the observation that when *Fram* left Christiania, fully loaded, in 1910, displacement was 1100 tons, and the ice skin showed only twelve and a half inches (32cm) above the water amidships. Over the deck was an arrangement of shelters and netting, to protect the dogs on their long journey south, and there were additions on the inside too: the cabins were decorated with photographs, provided by King Haakon and Queen Maud of Norway, and with embroidery given by the women of Horten. Amundsen was amused to find visitors to the ship talking of boudoirs when they entered the cabin.

Sverdrup's modifications had increased the *Fram*'s accommodation, but by all accounts, for this voyage the ship was full to bursting. First Lieutenant Thorvald Nilsen, who captained the ship, lists the living creatures on board as "nineteen men, ninety-seven dogs, four pigs, six carrier pigeons, and one canary" (*The South Pole*, 367); the canary was named Fridtjof, in honour of Nansen. There were also the sleds, dog harnesses, skis, ski poles, snow shoes, as well as supplies like coal, oil, timber, and 42 cases full of things like books, and other luxuries. Amundsen gathered a collection of Antarctic literature, books written by explorers from Sir James Clark Ross, to Scott and Ernest Shackleton, adding up to a library of almost 3000 volumes.

Many individuals and businesses donated supplies to the expedition. There were enough cigars for each man to smoke one on Saturday evenings, and after Sunday lunch, and there were donated supplies of sweets, chocolate, fruit syrups, biscuits, cheese, sugar, tea, and coffee, to supplement the tinned pemmican (a combination of dried meat and lard) which would be their principle diet. Yet another firm supplied five years' worth of soap.

Amundsen also allowed each man one dram and fifteen drops of rum at dinner on Wednesday and Sundays, and a glass of Toddy on Saturday evening. The subject of alcohol on Polar expeditions was much disputed, but while alcoholic drinks were forbidden on sledge journeys, for reasons of weight, Amundsen had a liberal view on board ship, and in winter quarters: "Personally I regard alcohol, used in moderation, as a medicine in Polar regions … A tot of spirits is often a very good thing when one goes below after a bitter watch on deck and is just turning in." (*The South Pole*, 53-54)

The declared purpose of the voyage, when *Fram* sailed from Norway on June 7, 1910, was to conduct oceanographical experiments in the North Atlantic. These experiments were taken seriously, but they also allowed thorough sea trials for the ship. After three weeks' sailing, *Fram* called at Bergen, where the troublesome engine was stripped down, rebuilt, and refueled with paraffin. In his account of the voyage, Nilsen claims this did the trick, and the engine gave no further trouble.

After a short stop at Christiansand, where the dogs and their supplies came on board, *Fram* departed on August 9, to the sound of the Norwegian national anthem, played by the bands of warships in the harbour. From there it took almost a month to reach the island of Madeira, where the expedition stayed for a few days. The ship's propeller was overhauled, and the men entertained themselves, descending from the hills above the town of Funchal on sledges. It was during this short stopover that Amundsen revealed his new plans, though the canine deck cargo, the southerly course, and the general outfitting of the ship, must have given the crew some idea where they were going.

Local journalists on the island certainly assumed the *Fram*'s destination was Antarctica, but to Amundsen's relief the news did not spread beyond Madeira until after they had left. From Madeira he sent the now famous telegram to Scott: "Beg leave to inform you *Fram* proceeding Antarctic. Amundsen." They set sail again on September 9.

Fram's curved hull was strong enough to have survived several winters beset in the Arctic ice, but the design had known disadvantages in the open sea. Even Nansen had described the ship as "a log" in open water. Once south of the Equator and into the 'Roaring Forties' it became clear that the ship rolled continually in an unusual, and uncomfortable way, especially when confronted with heavy seas. Nilsen describes the dogs sliding around on the deck, rolling into one another, and fighting. Even so, he declared the *Fram* a "first-rate sea boat, [which] hardly ships any water" (*The South Pole*, 368). Amundsen was also impressed, declaring, with one eye on his critics, and another on Nansen, that although "The ship was no racer, nor was she a log" (68).

By the beginning of January 1911, they were among icebergs, and managed to kill a seal to feed the dogs, and themselves. Then, on January 11, they saw the Ross Ice Barrier, a hundred miles long and towering hundreds of feet high. Amundsen describes it:

"At 2.30 p.m. We came in sight of the Great Ice Barrier. Slowly it rose up out of the sea until we were face to face with it in all its imposing majesty. It is difficult with the help of the pen to give any idea of the impression this mighty wall of ice makes on the observer who is confronted with it

for the first time. It is altogether a thing which can hardly be described; but one can understand very well that this wall of 100 feet in height was regarded for a generation as an insuperable obstacle to further southward progress." (*The South Pole*, 105)

A few days after first sighting the Barrier, the expedition arrived at the natural harbour which was to be their landing point, and set about transferring the equipment, across the sea ice, to the Barrier itself. There they constructed a prefabricated hut, and established a base, 16,000 miles and five months' sailing from Norway. Such was his affection for the ship that Amundsen named the spot Framheim.

By January 16, camps had been set up on the ice, and the expedition began moving boxes, sledges, and supplies up to Framheim. As the sea ice melted and broke up, the *Fram* was brought right up to the edge of the Barrier, where, as Nilsen puts it "we lay in peace until we went for good" (*The South Pole*, 373). In the mean time, the *Fram* played host to a visiting party from the *Terra Nova*, who needed some convincing that it was in fact the *Fram*, and not a whaler. Both ships had attained the furthest south possible at that time, 78°38' South.

Before *Fram* left the Barrier, Amundsen gave Nilson his orders in the form of a letter: to sail first to Buenos Aires for repairs, fuel, and supplies, and from there to carry out oceanographical observations in the South Atlantic between South America and South Africa. Nilsen was to return with the *Fram* to the Ice Barrier to pick up the shore party, who by then would have returned to Framheim from the Pole. Amundsen was realistic about the plan, concluding:

"The sooner you can make your way to the Barrier in 1912, the better. I mention no time, as everything depends upon circumstances, and I leave it to you to act according to your judgement.

In all else that concerns the interests of the Expedition, I leave you entire freedom of action.

If on your return to the Barrier you should find that I am prevented by illness or death from taking over the leadership of the Expedition, I place this in your hands, and beg you most earnestly to endeavour to carry out the original plan of the Expedition—the exploration of the North Polar basin.

With thanks for the time we have spent together, and in the hope that when we meet again we shall have reached our respective goals." (*The South Pole*, 374)

The Voyage of the *Fram*

As planned, on February 15, 1911, *Fram* sailed for Buenos Aires, leaving Amundsen and the shore party to begin preparing for their long trek to the Pole. But before setting course for Argentina, Nilsen decided to head northeast along the Barrier, to explore an area Scott had previously named King Edward VII Land. The dangers in this kind of exploration quickly became apparent, as thick fog descended. Nilsen records how "All of a sudden we were close upon a lofty iceberg, so that we had to put the helm hard over to go clear", but he also remarks on the *Fram*'s handling: "The *Fram* steers splendidly, however, when she is in proper trim, and turns as if on a pivot; besides which, it was calm." (*The South Pole*, 375)

It was a lucky escape, and even though the weather improved, Nilsen gave up on his plan to explore, turned the *Fram* northwest into open water, and left the northern part of the Barrier uncharted. With only a third of the load with which they had left Norway, *Fram* made good progress in the breeze that sprang up on February 20, but Nilsen bemoaned the shortening days, especially amongst the drift ice. After leaving the Antarctic Circle, Nilsen hoped to confirm the existence of the Nimrod Islands, marked 'D' for 'Doubtful' on the charts. He, like others before and after, failed to find them, and he drew a moral for himself: "Don't go on voyages of discovery, my friend; you're no good at it!"

In the South Pacific, *Fram* began the familiar rolling "fandango" amid fields of icebergs, but on March 13 they were hit by what Nilsen called a hurricane. The barometer fell rapidly to 28.26 inches (718mm), and they took in sail, but the *Fram* proved more than a match for the wind, and the heavy sea:

"Finally *Fram* showed herself in all her glory as the best sea-boat in the world. It was extraordinary to watch how she behaved. Enormous seas came surging high to windward, and we, who were standing on the bridge, turned our backs to receive them, with some such remarks as: 'Ugh, that's a nasty one coming.' But the sea never came. A few yards from the ship it looked over the bulwarks and got ready to hurl itself upon her. But at the last moment the *Fram* gave a wriggle of her body and was instantly at the top of the wave, which slipped under the vessel. Can anyone be surprised if one gets fond of such a ship? Then she went down with the speed of lightning from the top of the wave into the trough, a fall of fourteen or fifteen yards.

When we sank like this, it gave one the same feeling as dropping from the twelfth to the ground-floor in an American express elevator, 'as if everything was coming up'." (*The South Pole*, 381)

Despite the violence of the storm, life below decks went on as normal, the cook whistling as he worked, and the canary singing. The last iceberg was seen on March 14, and *Fram* passed Cape Horn on March 31. Having estimated that the voyage from the Barrier to Buenos Aires would take two months, they arrived after 62 days at sea. By then, since leaving Norway, they had been almost round the world, and had not lowered anchor for seven months.

Since the plan was to sail the South Atlantic for three months, before returning to Buenos Aires for supplies, *Fram* left Argentina on June 8, 1911, aiming to return in early September. By then the ship would have covered a further 8,000 miles, visiting the coast of Africa, St. Helena, and Trinidad, taking water samples all the way. They measured the water temperature and different depths, and at stations around 100 miles apart, but the *Fram* was not ideal for this, rolling too much to make soundings easy. The ship also had "too little both of sail area and engine power" to maintain regular progress. Nevertheless, they took 891 samples of water, and sent 190 specimens of plankton back to Norway.

It was during this circuit around the South Atlantic that the *Fram* underwent repairs.

In the south-east trade wind, the engine was overhauled, and the ship cleaned, tarred, and painted. The rigging and sails were in need of constant repair. Nilsen notes in his account of the voyage that on June 30 the *Fram* "completed her first circumnavigation of the globe" when they crossed the path of the voyage from Norway to the Ice Barrier. They reached St. Helena as planned on July 29, and Trinidad on August 12, entering the Buenos Aires roads on September 1.

Short of money, with the *Fram* empty, and Amundsen's shore party still on the Ice Barrier, waiting for the moment when they would begin their march for the Pole, Nilsen had to ask for help from Don Pedro Christophersen, an expatriate Norwegian businessman. Despite the expedition's unpopularity, Christophersen not only paid for enough provisions to last a year, but promised to send a relief expedition, should *Fram* not return. By October 4, still two weeks before Amundsen even set out for the Pole, the ship was ready to leave the quay, which it now shared with the *Deutschland*, the ship of Wilhelm Filchner's unsuccessful German Antarctic expedition.

The journey back to the Barrier was a difficult one. The wind refused to co-operate, and the steady westerlies they needed were rare. But at least this time they carried sheep and pigs on board, so fresh food was abundant. Nilsen was relieved to find that the *Fram* was sailing better than in 1910, but the need to exploit the wind whenever they could led

to torn sails and broken rigging. On one occasion an empty water tank broke loose on deck, and was almost lost overboard. More frustrating, though, were the calms and headwinds, which forced them to run the engine incessantly. Christmas was celebrated in the cabin, which Nilsen had decorated with flags. Entertainments included music, and a dinner of soup, roast pork, potatoes, and whortleberries. They toasted "the King and Queen, Don Pedro Christophersen, Captain Amundsen, and the *Fram*" with aquavit and Norwegian Bock beer, before the engine was restarted at 10pm, and the journey resumed.

Before auxiliary engines were common, ships could not manoeuvre easily to escape becoming trapped in pack ice. The best whaling captains were those who could navigate paths through the ice, watching ahead as gaps opened and closed. In the early nineteenth century this meant long hours at the masthead calling out instructions to the helmsman, and a well drilled crew, able to act at once when a change of direction was needed. In his short account of the *Fram*'s voyage back to the Barrier, Nilsen speculates on the passage of Sir James Ross, who sailed twice to the Antarctic in the 1840s. Nilsen concludes that, without an engine, Ross must have found a place where ice was scarce, or else was lucky in finding a way through.

Fram did not have time to waste in investigating the route of Ross's voyage, and the engine made things easier: "We went simply at haphazard; now and then we were lucky enough to come to great open channels and even lakes, but then the ice closed again absolutely tight … The ice remained more or less close until we were right down in lat. 73°S. And long. 179°W" (*The South Pole*, 398).

Fram arrived back at the Barrier on January 8, 1912, and after fighting an easterly headwind, made it to the Bay of Whales. They found a spot not far from Framheim, where Amundsen and the shore party were expected. Nilsen calculated that they had covered a total distance of 25,000 miles since leaving Norway. *Fram* waited in the bay through most of January, drifting closer to Framheim as the ice broke up in the Antarctic summer. By January 25, when the triumphant Southern Party returned, the ship was very close. Famously, the crew of the *Fram*, and the men who had spent a year on shore, talked for an hour before Nilsen asked Amundsen: "Well, of course you have been at the South Pole?" The answer, of course, was that he had. Three days later, having loaded provisions onto the ship, the expedition set sail for Hobart, Tasmania.

Fram sailed into Hobart on March 7, where the provisions from Buenos Aires finally ran out. During the thirteen days the expedition stayed there, the ship was full of visitors. Douglas Mawson, whose own expedition was preparing to depart for Antartica, met with Amundsen and Nilsen. Like many expedition vessels Mawson's ship, the *Aurora* (built in 1876) was a former Dundee whaler and Canadian sealer, only recently retired from the

27

Newfoundland sealing fleet. Although by then *Aurora* was an old ship, it had a reputation for being able to resist the ice in much the same way as the *Fram*. In 1884, while assisting in the successful rescue of an American Arctic expedition, led by Adolphus Greely, *Aurora* was 'nipped' by ice in the Davis Strait. Anticipating disaster, the crew unloaded their things onto the ice, but to their astonishment, saw the ship lifted clear, and, when the ice receded, sink back into the water none the worse for the ordeal.

Mawson, who had turned down Scott's invitation to join his expedition, made a good choice of vessel, but despite her resilience, *Aurora* was lost in 1917, probably in the Southern Ocean. Notably, Greely was one of Nansen's greatest critics, insisting, before the first voyage of the *Fram*, across the Arctic icecap, that the ship would not survive.

Fram sailed back to Buenos Aires, by way of Cape Horn. and Nilsen's account ends with statistics of the famous voyage:

"Since *Fram* left Christiania on June 7, 1910, we have been two and a half times around the globe; the distance covered is about 54,400 nautical miles; the lowest reading of the barometer during this time was 27.56 inches (700 millimetres) in March, 1911, in the South Pacific, and the highest 30.82 inches (783 millimetres), in October, 1911, in the South Atlantic." (*The South Pole*, 403)

During the remaining part of 1912, 1913, and the spring of 1914, *Fram* stayed in the Tropics, while Amundsen went on a lecture tour of the United States. It was hoped that the *Fram* would be the first ship to navigate the Panama Canal, but delays made that impossible. *Fram* arrived back in Horten on July 16, 1914, but by then was in a state of serious neglect, and disrepair. Not long after *Fram*'s arrival in Norway, dry rot was discovered, putting an end to Amundsen's plans to repeat Nansen's drift expedition.

Amundsen's expedition returned having fulfilled its mission, and tributes were paid to a chief whose planning and leadership had taken his team to the Pole safely, and uneventfully. But this view of the Amundsen expedition is one largely attributable to Amundsen, whose 1912-1913 account quickly became the standard version of events. At Hobart, Amundsen had made the expedition members sign documents promising not to publish their own accounts. Expedition members received the Medal of the South Pole, from King Haakon VII of Norway. But Hjalmar Johansen, Nansen's companion on the first voyage of the *Fram* across the North Polar icecap, was not part of the celebrations. His sad story tells us something about Amundsen, and the mythology of the heroic age of exploration.

Johansen had been a member of an eight-man team which made an early assault on the South Pole, on September 8, 1911, and was beaten back by bad weather and temperatures below −50C (-58F). In the chaos of their return to Framheim, Johansen, a former gymnast, well known for his physical strength, rescued the young and inexperienced Kristian Prestrud, and carried him back to the hut in the dark. Johansen had been against the early start, and now, in front of the whole expedition, he accused Amundsen of having abandoned them. Amundsen, refusing to accept that this early attempt was badly planned, removed Johansen from the Pole team. Instead he was sent to explore Edward VII Land on a mission led by Prestrud, a humiliation in itself, since Johansen was much more experienced in polar exploration. At Hobart, Johansen was

THE "FRAM" AT THE ICE EDGE, JANUARY, 1912.

dismissed and instructed to find his own way home. He took his own life in 1913.

In 1911, *Fram*, with her wooden hull and rudimentary diesel engine, was a state of the art vessel, and a blueprint for later ships. Norwegian polar exploration vessel *Maud*, with which Amundsen sailed through the Northeast passage from Norway to Alaska, was built with *Fram* in mind. In turn *Maud* became the model for *St. Roch*, a Royal Canadian Mounted Police vessel, which became the first ship to navigate the Northwest Passage from west to east, in 1940-1944. *St. Roch*'s curved, ice-resisting hull, and her combination of sails and diesel engine, betray an obvious lineage from the revolutionary *Fram*.

After returning from Antarctica, *Fram* remained at Horten dockyard until 1929, when, after years of arguments, Otto Sverdrup, with Lars Christensen, and Oscar Wisting (who had been with Amundsen at the South Pole) headed a preservation effort. A year later, the ship was restored to its 1890s condition, but it was several more years before a permanent home was found. Sverdrup was instrumental in creating a museum for the *Fram*, on the Bygdøy Peninsula, which was finally opened, with the ship at its centre, on May 20, 1936. The building created to house the ship forms a giant A-frame, echoing the shape of an expeditionary tent. *Fram* has remained there ever since.

The heroic age of polar exploration reached its zenith a century ago with Amundsen's arrival at the South Pole, and while the romantic draw of the ice remains, the polar regions are now disputed territories in a battle between nation states, scientists, environmentalists, and the corporations drilling, and digging for oil and minerals. In the years since 2000, as the ice has retreated, the Arctic and Antarctic have become accessible to more people than before. Cruise ships full of tourists wielding cameras patrol amongst the icebergs. Where once explorers struggled with sleds and skis, where native people hunted and fished, and whalers lost ships and sailors to the ice, now icebreakers, and TV crews travel with relative ease. To look at *Fram* now is to see how far we have come in a technological sense, and yet also to realise how limited our field of view remains.

Fram Timeline

1881: American exploration vessel *Jeanette* wrecked off Siberia.

1884: Wreckage from the *Jeanette* found on the Greenland coast.

1890: Nansen's plan to 'sail' to the North Pole is made public in an address to the Christiania Geographical Society.

1891: Nansen publishes an article in *Naturen* outlining his plan.

1892: October 6. *Fram* is launched at Colin Archer's shipyard in Larvik.

1893: June 24. *Fram* departs from Christiania (Oslo). Arrived at Vardø, the last Norwegian port, on July 18.

September. *Fram* becomes trapped in the ice off Siberia at 78°49'N, 132°53'E.

1894: March 22. *Fram* passes the 80°N mark.

1895: January 3. *Fram* passes Greely's Farthest North record of 83°24'N

March 14. Nansen and Johansen set off with skis and dog sleds, seeking the North Pole. Otto Sverdrup, captain of the *Fram*, is appointed the expedition's leader.

April 7. Nansen and Johansen reach 86°13.6'N, a new Farthest North record.

November 15. *Fram* reaches 85°55'N, Farthest North for a vessel, and only 22 miles south of Nansen's new record.

1895-1896: *Fram* drifts with the ice, taking soundings of as much as 2,700m depth, proving that there is no polar landmass under the Arctic icecap.

1896: August 13. *Fram* reaches open water and heads for Norway. The crew are reunited with Nansen and Johansen at Tromsø, on August 21.

1896: September 9. The expedition arrives in Christiania to a rapturous reception. Nansen was invited to stay at the Royal Palace with his family.

1896-1898: *Fram* is in storage at the Horten naval dockyard.

1898: *Fram*'s freeboard (the distance from the waterline to the upper deck level) is increased to give more room, in preparation for Sverdrup's voyage to the Canadian Arctic Islands.

June 24. Sverdrup, with 16 others, sets off to chart the Arctic Islands, and to collect information about animals and plants.

1898-1902: *Fram* is beset in ice near Ellesmere Island, to the north west of Greenland. The expedition yielded thousands of botanical, geological and other samples, as well as information about the earth's magnetism. The results from the expedition were not published until 1919.

1902-1907: *Fram* is in storage at Horten dockyard.

1907: Roald Amundsen investigates using *Fram* for an Arctic expedition, with the aim of claiming the North Pole.

1908: *Fram* is inspected by Amundsen and Colin Archer, the ship's builder, and found to be repairable.

1909: The North Pole is claimed by Robert Peary (Frederick Cook's 1908 claim was by then discredited).

Fram is refurbished, repaired, and made ready for Amundsen's expedition. By 1909, Amundsen was chasing the South Pole, but the plan remained secret.

1910: June 7. *Fram* leaves Christiania to undertake oceanographical research in the North Atlantic. Returned to Bergen after a few weeks for engine repairs.

August 9. Sails from Christiansand with dogs and sleds on board.

September. *Fram* arrives at the island of Madeira, where Amundsen reveals his new plan. He sends a telegram to rival Robert Scott, telling him the *Fram* was heading for Antarctica.

1911: January. *Fram* arrives at the Great Ice Barrier, before sailing on to the Bay of Whales, where a base known as Framheim is established.

February 12. *Fram* leaves Framheim, and the shore party, and heads for Buenos Aires for supplies.

June-September. Oceanographical measurements in the South Atlantic.

October 4. *Fram* sails from Buenos Aires heading for Framheim.

1912: January 8. *Fram* arrives at Framheim.

January 25. The triumphant southern party return to Framheim, having been to the South Pole.

January 28. *Fram* leaves for Hobart, Tasmania.

March 7. Arrives at Hobart, where Amundsen announces that they have been to the South Pole. Hjalmar Johansen is dismissed and told to find his own way back to Norway.

Fram Sails back to Buenos Aires for supplies.

1912-1914: Amundsen goes on a lecture tour around the United States, and makes plans for the *Fram* to be the first ship through the Panama Canal. When this plan falls through, *Fram* returns to Norway.

1914: July 16. *Fram* arrives back at the Horten dockyard, where dry rot is discovered.

1914-1929: *Fram* is in storage at Horten, but is in serious decline.

1929: Otto Sverdrup, Lars Christensen, and Oscar Wisting campaign successfully to have the *Fram* restored to 1890 condition.

1836: May 20. Opening of the *Fram* museum, with the ship as its central, indoor exhibit, on the Bygdøy Peninsula, Oslo.

Technical Data

The *Fram*

Description: Three-masted fore-and-aft schooner, with an auxiliary steam engine rated at 220hp (replaced for the 1910 expedition with a diesel engine).

Length of keel: 31 metres (103.3 English feet).
Length of waterline: 34.5 metres (119 feet).
Overall length: 39 metres (128 feet).
Beam at waterline: 10.4 metres (34 feet).
Maximum beam: 11 metres (36 feet).
Depth: 5.25 metres (17.2 feet).
Displacement (draught of 4.75 metres, or 15.6 feet): 800 tons.
Weight: 402 gross tons register, 807 tons net.
Sail area: 600 square metres (6458 square feet).

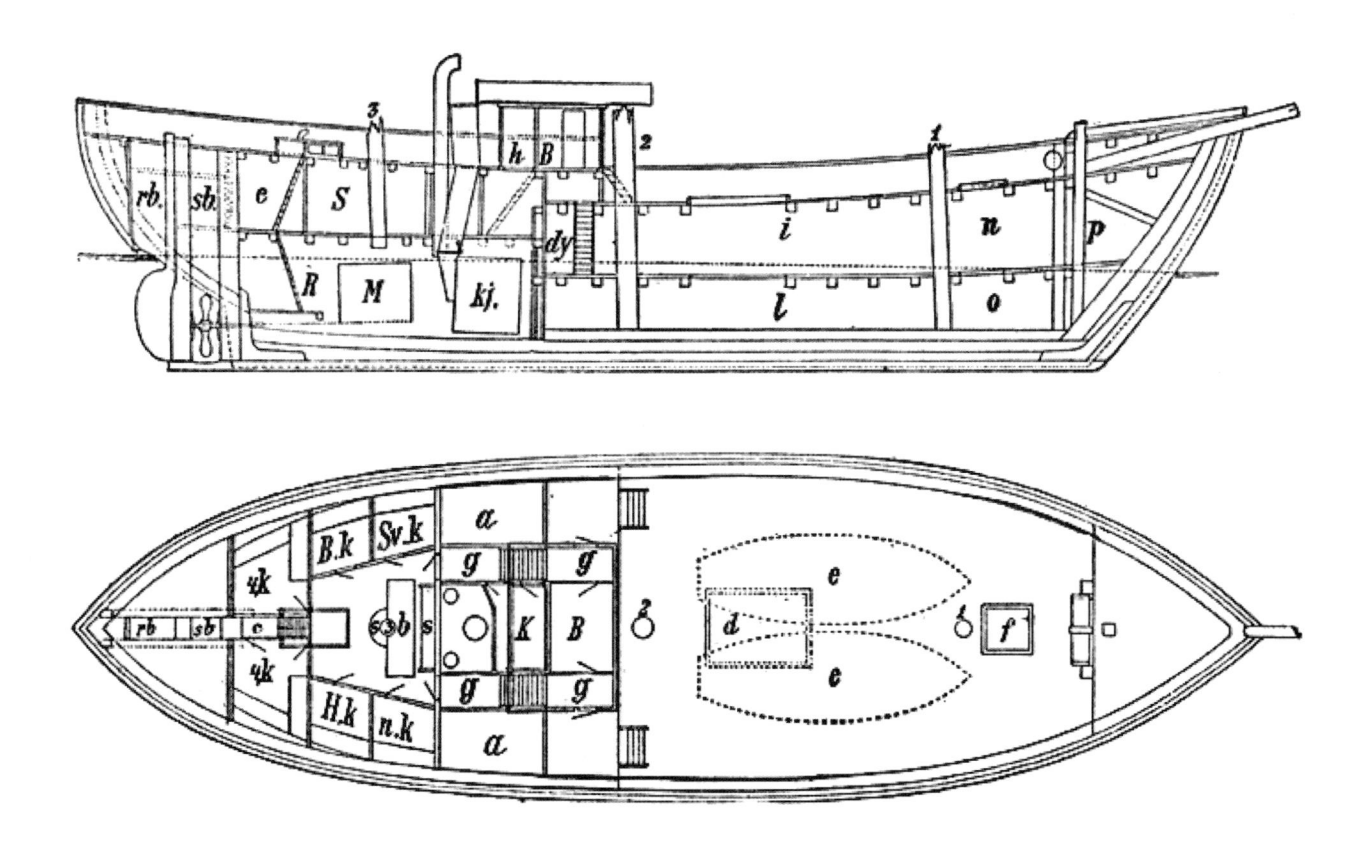

Bibliography

Amundsen, Roald. *The South Pole.* Translated from the Norwegian by A.G. Chater, 1912. Ebook edition used here in ePub format from http://www.gutenberg.org.

Fleming, Fergus. *Barrow's Boys.* London: Granta Books, 1998.

Jackson, C. Ian (ed.). *The Arctic Whaling Journals of William Scoresby the Younger. Vol. III, The Voyages of 1817, 1818, and 1820.* London: Ashgate for The Hakluyt Society, 2009.

Lainema, Matti, and Juha Nurminen. *A History of Arctic Exploration: Discovery, Adventure, and Endurance at the Top of the World.* London: Anova Books, 2009.

Nansen, Fridtjof. *Farthest North. Being the Record of a Voyage of Exploration of the Ship "Fram" 1893-96 and of a Fifteen Months' Sleigh Journey by Dr. Nansen and Lieut. Johansen.* London: Harper Brothers, 1897. Ebook edition used here in ePub format from http://www.gutenberg.org

New York Times. 'Will Nansen Come Back'. March 3, 1895. Accessed March 24, 2011.

Scoresby, William. *Voyage to the Whale Fishery, 1922.* First published, 1823. Edition used here, Whitby: Caedmon Reprints, 1980.

Useful Websites

Antarctic Circle. http://antarctic-circle.org Accessed March 24, 2011.
Fram Museum. http://www.frammuseum.no/ Accessed March 24, 2011.

Printed in Poland
by Amazon Fulfillment
Poland Sp. z o.o., Wrocław